Regions and Rivers of Georgia

Kathleen Kopp, M.S.Ed.

Consultants

Regina Holland, Ed.S., *Henry County Schools*
Christina Noblet, Ed.S., *Paulding County School District*
Jennifer Troyer, *Paulding County Schools*

Publishing Credits

Rachelle Cracchiolo, M.S.Ed., *Publisher*
Conni Medina, M.A.Ed., *Managing Editor*
Emily R. Smith, M.A.Ed., *Series Developer*
Diana Kenney, M.A.Ed., NBCT, *Content Director*
Torrey Maloof, *Editor*
Courtney Patterson, *Multimedia Designer*

Image Credits: p.2 D Ramey Logan/Wikimedia Commons; pp.12-13 Pamela J. W. Gore; p.15 JRC, Inc. / Alamy Stock Photo; p.17 Science Source, Randy Browning/U.S. Fish and Wildlife Service; p.19 RSBPhoto / Alamy Stock Photo, Wolfgang Kaehler/LightRocket via Getty Images, tomcat2170/Bigstock; p.20 James Randklev/CORBIS; p.23 RosalreneBetancourt 7 / Alamy Stock Photo; p.25 Timothy J. Carroll/Flickr; All other images from iStock and/or Shutterstock.

Library of Congress Cataloging-in-Publication Data

Names: Kopp, Kathleen, author.
Title: Regions and rivers of Georgia / Kathleen Kopp.
Description: Huntington Beach, CA : Teacher Created Materials, Inc., 2017. |
    Includes index.
Identifiers: LCCN 2015042451 | ISBN 9781493825509 (pbk.)
Subjects: LCSH: Georgia--Geography--Juvenile literature.
Classification: LCC F286.3 .K67 2017 | DDC 917.58--dc23
LC record available at http://lccn.loc.gov/2015042451

Teacher Created Materials
5301 Oceanus Drive
Huntington Beach, CA 92649-1030
http://www.tcmpub.com
ISBN 978-1-4938-2550-9
© 2017 Teacher Created Materials, Inc.
Printed in China
Nordica.082019.CA21901386

27

9

Table of Contents

17

Road Trip!

If you could go anywhere in Georgia, where would you go? Would you swim in the ocean? Would you take a hike in the woods? Would you fish on a lake?

In Georgia, you can do all of these things—and more! Georgia has shorelines, mountains, and lakes. There are forests and fields. It has rivers, rocks, and ridges. It is a beautiful state.

Greetings from GEORGIA

34 USA

Five Regions

The state of Georgia has five main **regions**. These are large areas of land. Each area has different features.

Each region has its own **landscape**. That is what the land looks like. Each region also has its own **climate**. That is what the weather is like. Plant and animal life can be different in each region, too.

Valley and Ridge

Coastal Plain

Appalachian (ap-puh-LAY-shuhn) Plateau

Blue Ridge Mountains

Piedmont (PEED-mahnt)

7

Appalachian Plateau

The Appalachian **Plateau** is in the northwest corner of the state. The Appalachian Mountain chain is long. It starts north of New York. It ends in Alabama. It helps form this region.

A plateau is an area of high, flat land. Because it is so high here, it is often colder than in the rest of the state. There may even be snow in the winter!

Appalachian Plateau

A Great View

From the top of Lookout Mountain, some say you can see seven states at one time!

Lookout Mountain

Blue Ridge Mountains

The Blue Ridge Mountains are part of the Appalachian chain. Blue Ridge has some of the tallest peaks in the chain. And they really do look blue!

This area gets a lot of rain. It's very wet there. The land is covered in forests. Black bears and wild boars roam the region. You may even see a turkey.

Blue Ridge Mountains

4,784 Feet!

The tallest mountain in Georgia is Brasstown Bald. It is 4,784 feet tall!

Valley and Ridge

This region is made up of valleys and ridges. A valley is the lowland between mountains. A ridge is an area of long, thin land at the top of a mountain.

The valleys have rich soil. They are perfect for farming. The ridges are covered in pine trees. This area has lots of caves. Frogs, snakes, and crayfish live in this region.

Valley and Ridge

Piedmont

The Piedmont region is in the center of the state. Many people live there. In fact, more people live there than in any other region.

There are low, rolling hills in this region. There are also many streams and rivers. There are even waterfalls! The soil here is red and rocky. You can see large rocks peeking out from under the ground.

Piedmont

downtown Atlanta

Stone Mountain is the world's largest piece of exposed granite.

Coastal Plain

The Coastal Plain is the largest region in the state. It stretches all the way to the Atlantic Ocean. The winters are mild there. But the summers are hot and humid. There are often thunderstorms, too. There can even be **hurricanes**!

The soil is made of sand and clay. It is not good for growing crops. Instead, people use the land to grow pine trees.

Coastal Plain

Fall Line

Old Coastline

The northern border of the Coastal Plain is the Fall Line. This is the prehistoric coastline!

longleaf pine

Exploring Rivers

Georgia has many rivers. They twist and turn their way through the state. They help shape the land.

The Ocmulgee (ohk-MUHL-gee) River starts near Atlanta. It moves quickly over rocks as it flows south. Then, it reaches the Coastal Plain and slows down. It meets with the Oconee (oh-KOH-nee) River at a place called the Forks. There, a new river starts!

High Falls State Park

Chattahoochee (chat-tuh-WHO-chee)

Oconee

Savannah

Altamaha (AWL-tuh-muh-haw)

Flint

St. Marys

the Forks

Ocmulgee

The Altamaha River starts at the Forks. It winds to the Atlantic Ocean. This area is full of swamps. Look out! Alligators hide there. And snakes lurk in the water.

Savannah River

The Savannah River starts in the Blue Ridge Mountains. It rolls from the mountains to the ocean. There is a large city near the **mouth** of the river. Do you know its name? It's Savannah!

The Chattahoochee River is very old. It starts high in the Blue Ridge Mountains. It flows southwest. People have lived on its **banks** for thousands of years.

Painted Rock

The Chattahoochee River's name comes from Creek Indian words meaning "painted rock."

The Flint River is long. It flows for about 350 miles. It starts in the Piedmont region. There, it is **groundwater**. Next, it moves south. It goes under Hartsfield-Jackson Airport. Then, it runs across the Coastal Plain.

These people paddle down the Flint River.

The St. Marys River is small. But it plays a big role. It acts as a border. It runs between Georgia and Florida.

The St. Marys River starts in the Okefenokee (oh-kuh-feh-NOH-kee) Swamp. It flows east. It heads toward the Atlantic Ocean. It is a "blackwater" stream. The water is clean. But it looks like dark tea.

Georgia

Okefenokee Swamp

St. Marys River

Florida

Georgia on My Mind

Georgia has many landscapes. There is a lot to see and do. Sniff the salty sea air as you walk along the coast. Take in the views from the mountains.

There is a famous song called "Georgia on My Mind." Next time you take a trip through the state, play it. Try to figure out why it is the state's song. It won't take you long!

Helton Creek Fall

Jekyll Island

Cloudland Canyon

Justify It!

Your friend's family wants to visit one region of Georgia. They want to hike in the woods. Which region would best suit their needs?

Write an argument about which region would be best. Justify your argument with evidence from the book.

Glossary

banks—areas of higher ground that run along the edge of a river

climate—the usual type of weather a place gets

groundwater—water that is underground

hurricanes—powerful and destructive storms with high winds

landscape—an area of land that looks a certain way

mouth—the place where a river meets the ocean

plateau—a large area of flat land that is higher than the land around it

regions—parts of an area that are different than other parts in some way

Index

Your Turn!

Are You Ready for an Adventure?

   Georgia is a state that offers many things to do.
It is a place where you can go on an adventure. Map
out three adventures through the regions of Georgia.
Explain why these adventures would be exciting.